The Little Flower

Student Workbook

Cataloging-in-Publication data on file with the Library of Congress.

Cover and interior design by Caroline Kiser

Arranged and edited by Jessica Grabowski and Brian Kennelly

Cover illustration by Gedge Harmon

ISBN: 978-1-5051-0709-8

Printed and bound in the United States of America

The Little Flower

Student Workbook

a comprehensive companion to the book by

Mary Fabyan Windeatt

TAN · BOOKS

Key Terms

These are important people, places, and things you should remember from this chapter.

Alençon the city in France where the Martin family lived

Louis Joseph Aloysius Stanislaus Martin Therese's father

Zelie Marie Guerin Therese's mother

Rose Taillé the woman who took care of baby Therese and who the baby mistook for her mother

Watchmaker the profession of Therese's father

Vocabulary

Read the sentences below, and note the use of the word in **bold**. *Write a definition or synonym for this word by considering its context.*

1. "My business is **prospering**, too. Why should we complain?"

2. "What is it, Papa?" Marie asked **anxiously**.

3. She had never seen such a poor little scrap of **humanity**.

4. They were deeply **afflicted** at the loss of their two sons.

Comprehension Questions

To better understand this chapter, ask yourself these questions, and write down your answers using complete sentences.

1. Why did people think the marriage of Louis Martin and Marie Guerin was a mistake?

2. How many children were born into the Martin family?

3. What was the first name of all the Martin children? Why did their parents name them this?

4. Where was Therese sent as a baby to improve her health?

5. When Therese was nearly five months old, she was healthy enough to return home. What happened when she was brought back to the Martin family?

Activity

The following is an optional activity used to help your comprehension of the text. Answer the questions and locate the answers in the Word Search.

1. the city in France where the Martin family lived at the time
2. the seventh child born to the Martin family, Marie ___________
3. The babies who died were likely with ________ in heaven.
4. The fourth child was Marie __________ who died at five years old.
5. The second son born to the Martin family was Marie ___________ __________.
6. The first son born to the Martin family was Marie _____________ ___________.
7. The third daughter born to the Martin family was Marie ___________.
8. the name of Therese's father
9. the oldest child in the Martin family who was the only who went by her first name
10. The eighth child born to the Martin family, who died as a baby, was named Marie ___________.
11. the second child born to the Martin family, Marie ___________
12. the woman who took care of Therese as a baby
13. the child born on January 2, 1873
14. the name of Therese's mother

Using your answers to the questions from the opposite page as your word bank, locate the answers within the Word Search.

E	C	R	L	L	P	W	K	H	J	D	G	L	J	Q
Q	N	F	K	V	O	N	Q	O	A	L	D	L	O	B
E	Z	I	F	A	T	Y	S	J	Q	O	B	U	S	S
F	R	D	L	K	D	E	C	S	G	H	S	U	E	O
K	R	G	I	U	P	W	M	R	X	X	E	K	P	M
G	K	C	K	H	A	R	S	U	W	V	E	X	H	L
I	H	A	J	M	P	P	O	Z	G	S	E	L	L	H
P	Q	O	A	E	E	J	J	C	E	R	S	O	O	G
U	H	R	E	I	L	E	Z	R	E	E	O	U	U	H
N	I	T	N	N	O	T	E	P	N	L	R	I	I	G
E	O	C	T	A	W	H	C	S	N	E	I	S	S	R
L	S	R	E	L	T	I	Z	D	C	Z	L	N	A	J
N	O	C	N	E	L	A	L	E	O	N	I	E	E	N
M	O	Z	I	M	L	T	I	X	Z	K	Q	F	H	S
T	G	T	G	A	C	G	T	T	O	G	W	Z	I	D

Note: *Some words may appear backwards.*

Key Terms

These are important people, places, and things you should remember from this chapter.

Les Mans The Martin girls attended a boarding school in this city.

Visitation convent the boarding school Marie and Pauline attended

Sister Mary Dosithée Zelie's sister who was at the Visitation convent and passed away before Zelie became sick

Lisieux the city where Zelie's brother lived

Isidore Guerin Zelie's brother, a chemist

Lourdes the place where Therese's mother and sisters made a pilgrimage in order to ask the Blessed Virgin Mary to intercede for their mother's health

Vocabulary

Read the sentences below, and note the use of the word in **bold**. *Write a definition or synonym for this word by considering its context.*

1. Mama had no use for such **nonsense**, but finally she had to agree that Papa had been right.

2. They **labored** in their own homes and brought in their pieces of lace at regular intervals.

3. I had no wish to **grieve** the Little Jesus.

4. Mama gave her an **affectionate** smile, then turned to me.

Comprehension Questions

To better understand this chapter, ask yourself these questions, and write down your answers using complete sentences.

1. What job did Therese's mother do before she was married? How did Therese's father come to help with this?

   ....

   ....

   ....

2. What did Therese's eldest sister, Marie, do when she finished her studies at Visitation convent?

   ....

   ....

   ....

3. Shortly after Therese turned four, what news did her mother receive?

   ....

   ....

   ....

4. Who did Therese's mother visit in Lisieux? What was his occupation?

   ....

   ....

   ....

5. Where did Therese's mother go on a pilgrimage? Who went with her?

   ....

   ....

   ....

Key Terms

These are important people, places, and things you should remember from this chapter.

Last Sacraments final sacraments received by a Catholic before death, including Confession, receiving the Eucharist, and Extreme Unction

Lisieux the place the Martin family moved after the death of their mother

Isidore Guerin the Martin girls' uncle

Aunt Celine married to Isidore; aunt to the Martin girls

Les Buissonnets new home to the Martin family, meaning "a wooded estate"

Bluebeard a make-believe person who frightened Therese

Vocabulary

Read the sentences below, and note the use of the word in **bold**. *Write a definition or synonym for this word by considering its context.*

1. This made us feel like little **exiles**, particularly on those mornings when we did not have enough time to say our prayers before leaving.

2. Nor could I **unburden** myself to anyone.

3. Accordingly, a house was **purchased** in Lisieux and in November of that same year, 1877, we said farewell to Alencon.

4. "I enjoyed the daily **excursions** with Papa after lessons were over, but the favorite day of the week for me was Sunday."

Comprehension Questions

To better understand this chapter, ask yourself these questions, and write down your answers using complete sentences.

1. What were Therese and Celine shy about at the neighbor's house?

2. Where did the Martin family move after the death of their mother? Who would they now be living near?

3. What kind of home did the Martin family move to? Why was it called *Les Buissonnets*?

4. After her first confession, Therese had Father Ducellier bless her rosary. Why was she disappointed after he did this?

5. What small sacrifice did Pauline ask Therese to make to teach her about sacrifices?

Key Terms

These are important people, places, and things you should remember from this chapter.

Victoria the Martin family's maid

Benedictine convent the place where Therese went to study just before the age of nine

Father Domin the Benedictine convent chaplain

hermit a person who lives in seclusion from the rest of the world

Carmelite nun a cloistered nun who lives with her community inside walls set apart from the rest of the world

Sister Agnes of Jesus the name Pauline took when she became a Carmelite nun

Vocabulary

Read the sentences below, and note the use of the word in **bold**. *Write a definition or synonym for this word by considering its context.*

1. Victoria was **indignant**.
2. Some of the girls, jealous that a nine-year-old should be in their class, **plagued** me and made me miserable.
3. In my own simple way, I thought it was God's Will that I suffer their **taunts**.
4. Then sudden **calamity** struck as Marie and I bumped into a display of vegetables outside a grocery store.

Comprehension Questions

To better understand this chapter, ask yourself these questions, and write down your answers using complete sentences.

1. Where did Therese attend school? How old was she?

2. Did Therese enjoy school? Was she a good student?

3. What did Therese's sister Pauline decide to do while Therese was in school?

4. What happened when Papa, Leonie and Marie went to Paris for Holy Week?

5. When Therese relapsed into illness again, how was it different?

Activity

The following is an optional activity used to help your comprehension of the text. Answer the questions, and locate the answers in the Word Search.

1. the home of the Martin Family in Lisieux
2. Therese's nickname given by her father
3. the maid of the Martin family at The Elms
4. All of the Martin girls studied at the ______________ convent.
5. The convent chaplain was ___________ ___________.
6. a cousin of the Martins who had the same name as the eldest Martin
7. the other cousin of the Martins who went to school with Celine and Therese
8. Marie and Therese pretended to be ___________ when they ran into a vegetable display.
9. Pauline decided to become a ____________ nun.
10. Mother Mary Gonzales was the __________ of the Carmelite convent.
11. Pauline took the name of Sister _________ of Jesus when she became a Carmelite nun.
12. Uncle _________ sent word to Therese's father and sister when she fell ill.
13. Therese's father sent word to have a ___________ of Masses said for her.
14. Upon Therese's miraculous recovery, the statue of the Blessed __________ smiled at her.
15. Therese believed her recovery was truly a ____________ and told no one of it.

Using your answers to the questions from the opposite page as your word bank, locate the answers within the Word Search.

Y	G	J	A	N	E	I	F	L	J	B	Q	A	Q	I
E	I	T	M	K	Q	H	V	Q	E	C	M	I	S	S
U	T	H	E	E	L	M	S	N	O	P	Y	R	Q	I
H	N	I	M	O	D	R	E	H	T	A	F	O	P	D
W	E	J	L	Y	F	D	Z	S	L	M	S	T	L	O
T	A	R	Z	E	I	R	S	R	I	E	M	C	I	R
B	X	R	M	C	M	E	R	R	N	C	F	I	T	E
S	X	Y	T	I	R	R	A	G	P	E	V	V	T	G
N	A	I	N	O	T	C	A	X	E	P	Y	Q	L	W
Q	N	L	I	I	L	S	L	C	I	N	P	W	E	L
E	Z	R	E	E	G	U	D	T	R	J	P	Q	Q	Q
Y	P	S	C	E	U	R	Y	H	A	B	U	H	U	Q
A	N	E	V	O	N	H	I	T	M	V	D	T	E	S
Y	X	E	M	V	V	Z	K	V	B	J	X	I	E	R
T	H	V	I	I	C	Y	T	H	Y	Q	K	L	N	J

Note: *Some words may appear backwards.*

Key Terms

These are important people, places, and things you should remember from this chapter.

first Holy Communion the sacrament of receiving Jesus in the Eucharist for the first time

Act of Consecration the solemn dedication Therese made to give herself and all her actions and deeds to the Blessed Virgin

Sacrament of Confirmation the sacrament of renewing one's baptismal promise and receiving the Holy Spirit, which leads to a firm profession of faith

Memorare a prayer to the Blessed Virgin Mary

Vocabulary

Read the sentences below, and note the use of the word in **bold**. *Write a definition or synonym for this word by considering its context.*

1. Soon I became confused and tearful, for now the miracle had become a source of **scruples**.

2. Because of it many people thought I was an **obstinate** child who delighted in being the center of attraction.

3. What a **dreadful** thing to be a sinner!

4. I tried to be very busy with my lessons, but all these **flattering** remarks reached my ears.

Comprehension Questions

To better understand this chapter, ask yourself these questions, and write down your answers using complete sentences.

1. Who did Therese tell about the miracle that took place? Who else found out?

2. How did Therese react to all the questions the nuns at Carmel asked about her vision of Our Lady?

3. How did Therese act differently from her classmates when she received her first Holy Communion?

4. After receiving her first Holy Communion, what resolutions did Therese make?

5. What gift did Therese pray to receive? When was this prayer answered?

Activity

The following is an optional activity meant to help you in your own prayer life.

1. Look up the words to the *Memorare,* and write out the prayer on the next page.

2. Pray the *Memorare.*

The Memorare

QUIZ 1

Chapters 1–5

Name ____________________ Date ______________ Score _______

Vocabulary

Complete the crossword puzzle using the definitions and synonyms below as clues. All answers will come from the vocabulary sections covered so far. Look back over these sections if you need assistance completing the puzzle. This should be the only part of the quiz where you can view your notes from previous sections.

1 point each (15 points total)

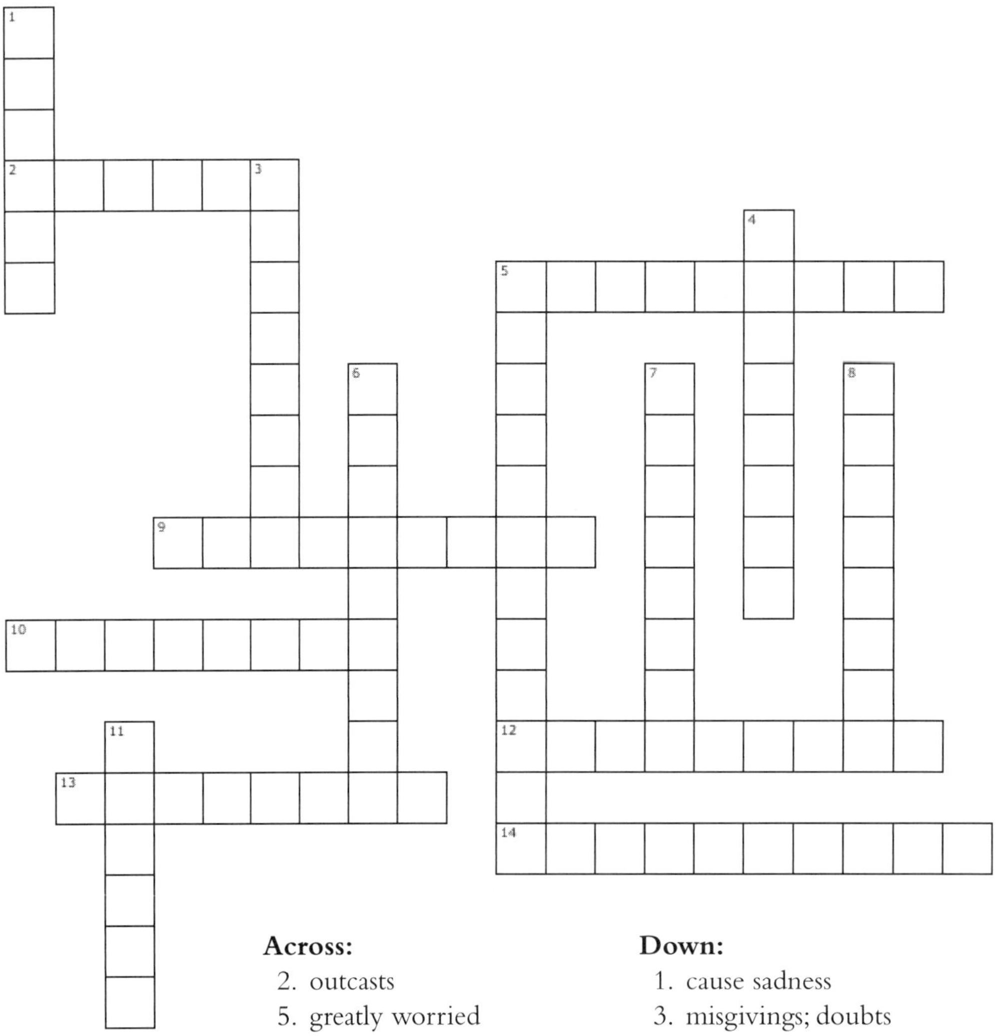

Across:

2. outcasts
5. greatly worried
9. stubborn
10. relieve one's feelings
12. feeling suffering
13. disaster
14. outings, short trip or journey

Down:

1. cause sadness
3. misgivings; doubts
4. the state of being human
5. loving
6. angry; feeling wrongly-accused
7. horrible
8. silly behavior or idea
11. insults

Key Terms

Match the correct term to its definition.

2 points each (50 points total)

_____ the city in France where the Martin family first lived
_____ the place the Martin family moved after the death of their mother
_____ Therese's Mother
_____ married to Isidore; aunt to the Martin girls
_____ a make-believe person who frightened Therese
_____ Zelie's brother; a chemist.
_____ new home to the Martin family meaning "a wooded estate"
_____ the city where the boarding school that the Martin girls went to was located
_____ the place where Therese's mother and sisters made a pilgrimage
_____ the sacrament of receiving Jesus in the Eucharist
_____ Therese preformed this act to dedicate herself to the Blessed Virgin
_____ the sacrament of renewing one's promise at Baptism
_____ a prayer to the Blessed Virgin Mary
_____ the woman who took care of baby Therese
_____ Zelie's sister
_____ the boarding school that the Martin girls attended
_____ full name of Therese's Father
_____ the profession of Therese's father
_____ the Martin family's maid
_____ the place where Therese went to study just before the age of nine
_____ the Benedictine convent chaplain
_____ a person who lives in seclusion from the rest of the world
_____ final sacrament received by a Catholic before death
_____ a cloistered nun who lives with her community
_____ the name Pauline took when she became a Carmelite

A. Act of Consecration
B. Alencon
C. Aunt Celine
D. Benedictine convent
E. Bluebeard
F. Carmelite nun
G. Father Domin
H. first Holy Communion
I. hermit
J. Isidore Guerin
K. Last Sacraments
L. Les Buissonnet
M. Les Mans
N. Lisieux
O. Louis Joseph Aloysius Stanislaus Martin
P. Lourdes
Q. Memorare
R. Rose Tallié
S. Sister Agnes of Jesus
T. Sister Mary Dosithée
U. the Sacrament of Confirmation
V. Victoria
W. Visitation convent
X. Watchmaker
Y. Zelie Marie Guerin

Multiple Choice

Choose the correct response and circle the answer.

2 points each (20 points total)

1. Why did people think the marriage of Louis Martin and Marie Guerin was a mistake?
   a. They were too young.
   b. They may have had religious vocations.
   c. They did not love each other.
   d. They were already married.

2. What were Therese and Celine shy about at the neighbor's house?
   a. playing outdoors
   b. eating their food
   c. saying prayers
   d. taking a nap

3. How old was Therese when she began to attend school?
   a. just before age 9
   b. just before age 5
   c. just before age 3
   d. just before age 11

4. Who took care of Therese as a baby?
   a. a farm woman
   b. her grandmother
   c. her mother
   d. her sister

5. What did Therese's father want to build for her when she was one year old?
   a. a tree house
   b. a canoe
   c. a wagon
   d. a swing

6. How did Therese act differently from her classmates when she received her first Holy Communion?
   a. She sang.
   b. She cried.
   c. She laughed.
   d. She fainted.

7. What kind of home did the Martin family move to?
   a. a beach house
   b. a mountain cottage
   c. a town home
   d. a wooded estate

8. What job did Therese's mother do before she was married?
   a. chef
   b. lace-maker
   c. secretary
   d. watchmaker

9. After receiving her first Holy Communion, what was one prayer Therese promised to pray daily?
   a. Our Father
   b. Hail Mary
   c. Memorare
   d. Angelus

10. Who miraculously saved Therese from her illness when she was a young girl?
    a. Saint Agnes
    b. her sisters
    c. the Blessed Virgin
    d. Mother Mary Gonzaga

Narration Exercise

The remaining 15 points of the quiz will come from this narration exercise. Answer the question below in 2–3 complete sentences.

What analogy did Therese's sister, Pauline, use to explain the complete happiness of all those who were in heaven?

Key Terms

These are important people, places, and things you should remember from this chapter.

Midnight Mass a vigil Mass said at midnight on Christmas Eve

Poor Clares an order of nuns (Leonie entered this order)

Canon Delatroette the priest who watched over the affairs of the Carmel community

Bishop of Bayeux the bishop of the diocese of Bayeux and Lisieux who could grant Therese permission to become a Carmelite at a young age

Pranzini a horrible criminal who lived in France at the time

Vocabulary

Read the sentences below, and note the use of the word in **bold**. *Write a definition or synonym for this word by considering its context.*

1. I was struck with an **intense** desire to stand in spirit at the foot of the Cross to receive this Blood and pour It out upon sinners.

2. When the opportunity arose to teach Catechism to two little girls, I **seized** it eagerly.

3. I marveled at my sister's **generosity**.

4. Such **criticism** and misunderstanding.

5. I clasped my hands **fervently** and turned an imploring glance upon the Bishop.

Comprehension Questions

To better understand this chapter, ask yourself these questions, and write down your answers using complete sentences.

1. How did Therese feel when she saw the picture of the Crucifixion?

....

....

....

2. What other vocation did Therese consider?

....

....

....

3. What vocations were Celine and Leonie considering?

....

....

....

4. What did Therese's father say they would do after Canon Delatroette told Therese she was too young to enter Carmel?

....

....

....

5. What was the outcome of the meeting with the Bishop about Therese entering Carmel?

....

....

....

CHAPTER 7

Disappointment in Rome

Key Terms

These are important people, places, and things you should remember from this chapter.

Our Lady of Victories a small church in Paris where a novena of Masses was offered for Therese while she was ill

Basilica of the Sacred Heart a basilica in Paris

Coliseum a site of games and entertainments for the pagans of ancient Rome

Martyr someone who dies for his or her faith

Catacombs underground tombs in Rome

Eternal City a nickname for the city of Rome

Pope Leo XIII the pope who Therese met on her pilgrimage to Rome

Vocabulary

Read the sentences below, and note the use of the word in **bold**. *Write a definition or synonym for this word by considering its context.*

1. Our Lady had really **restored** my health.

2. In the days that followed we were constantly exclaiming at the many **splendors** about us.

3. I was doing right to **abandon** myself to Him.

4. Every action proclaimed his deep **piety**, his genuine faith.

5. Then with all the **fervor** I could command, I tried again.

Comprehension Questions

To better understand this chapter, ask yourself these questions, and write down your answers using complete sentences.

1. What favor did Therese ask Mary when she was visiting Our Lady of Victories?

2. What did Therese see when she visited Loreto?

3. What did Celine and Therese do when they visited the Coliseum?

4. What did Therese do while visiting the Basilica of the Holy Cross of Jerusalem?

5. What did the pope say when Therese asked if she could enter Carmel at fifteen?

Key Terms

These are important people, places, and things you should remember from this chapter.

Holy Land the old land of Israel

Mother Mary Gonzaga the prioress at Carmel when Therese entered

Mother Mary of Angels the sub-prioress and novice mistress at Carmel

Father Pichon a priest familiar to the Martin family and confessor of Therese

The Imitation of Christ a Catholic devotional book that Therese read and loved

Vocabulary

Read the sentences below, and note the use of the word in **bold**. *Write a definition or synonym for this word by considering its context.*

1. On January 1, 1888 Mother Mary Gonzaga sent word that the bishop now authorized her to receive me as a **postulant**.

2. I understood Leonie's **anxiety**, and I assured her that every day I was praying for grace and strength to be a good religious.

3. Sometimes Marie and Pauline were **irritated** with me too.

4. I was greatly **consoled**, and promised not to worry anymore.

Comprehension Questions

To better understand this chapter, ask yourself these questions, and write down your answers using complete sentences.

1. Why was Leonie so worried about Therese entering the convent at Carmel?

   ....

   ....

   ....

2. Did Therese like the life of a Carmelite? What did she like or dislike about it?

   ....

   ....

   ....

3. What troubles did Therese face upon entering Carmel?

   ....

   ....

   ....

4. Did Therese seek out her sisters Marie and Pauline for help when going through the hard times?

   ....

   ....

   ....

5. Which priest finally put Therese at ease about her desire to be a saint?

   ....

   ....

   ....

Key Terms

These are important people, places, and things you should remember from this chapter.

Notre Dame a church in Alençon where Louis Martin visited

Sister Therese of the Child Jesus Therese's name as a Carmelite

Clothing Day the day one takes the habit of Carmel and makes a commitment

Sister Saint Peter an old nun with rheumatism who needed assistance

Vocabulary

Read the sentences below, and note the use of the word in **bold**. *Write a definition or synonym for this word by considering its context.*

1. The three of us stared in **bewilderment**.

2. Now, I **glimpsed** the truth.

3. This was a dreadful cross, one full of suffering and **humiliation**.

4. Wasn't it the coin with which sinners could be **ransomed**?

Comprehension Questions

To better understand this chapter, ask yourself these questions, and write down your answers using complete sentences.

1. For what small miracle did Therese pray for on her Clothing Day? Was it granted?

2. What tragedy occurred after Therese's Clothing Day?

3. What new duties were given to Therese? Why were these new duties especially difficult?

4. Who was Therese assigned to help? Why was this task difficult?

5. Therese was looking forward to her Religious Profession. Why did this not happen in January as planned?

Key Terms

These are important people, places, and things you should remember from this chapter.

Religious Profession one's solemn and permanent admission into a religious order

Visitation Order a female religious order that Therese prayed Leonie would enter

purgatory a place of temporal punishment for souls that are not entirely free of venial sins and must be cleansed before entering heaven

Vocabulary

Read the sentences below, and note the use of the word in **bold**. *Write a definition or synonym for this word by considering its context.*

1. No longer would I work with Pauline in the **refectory**.

2. From now on I was to be assistant sacristan, seeing that the altar linens and **vestments** used by the chaplain were kept in good order.

3. My eyes had shown at the exciting **prospect**, and I was just on the point of saying "Yes" when Marie interrupted.

4. I stood by in silent **admiration**.

Comprehension Questions

To better understand this chapter, ask yourself these questions, and write down your answers using complete sentences.

1. What did Therese write in her letter to the Lord while she waited for her Religious Profession?

2. What happened when Therese and all the Carmel nuns were silently praying on the eve of Therese's profession?

3. Therese stopped working in the refectory and was assigned a new task. What was it?

4. How did the influenza epidemic that broke out in Lisieux affect those at Carmel?

5. Who became the new prioress in February, 1893? Who else was appointed?

Activity

The following is an optional activity meant to help you in your own prayer life.

Therese was privileged to draw holy cards and write prayers.

On the next page, design and draw your own holy card of Our Lord, the Blessed Virgin, or a saint.

Write a simple prayer to go with it.

FRONT
Draw your image of Our Lord, the Blessed Virgin, or a saint.

BACK
Write out a prayer to go with your holy card.

Name_________________________ Date ____________________ Score_______

Vocabulary

Complete the crossword puzzle using the definitions and synonyms below as clues. All answers will come from the vocabulary sections covered so far. Look back over these sections if you need assistance completing the puzzle. This should be the only part of the quiz where you can view your notes from previous sections.

.5 point each (9 points total)

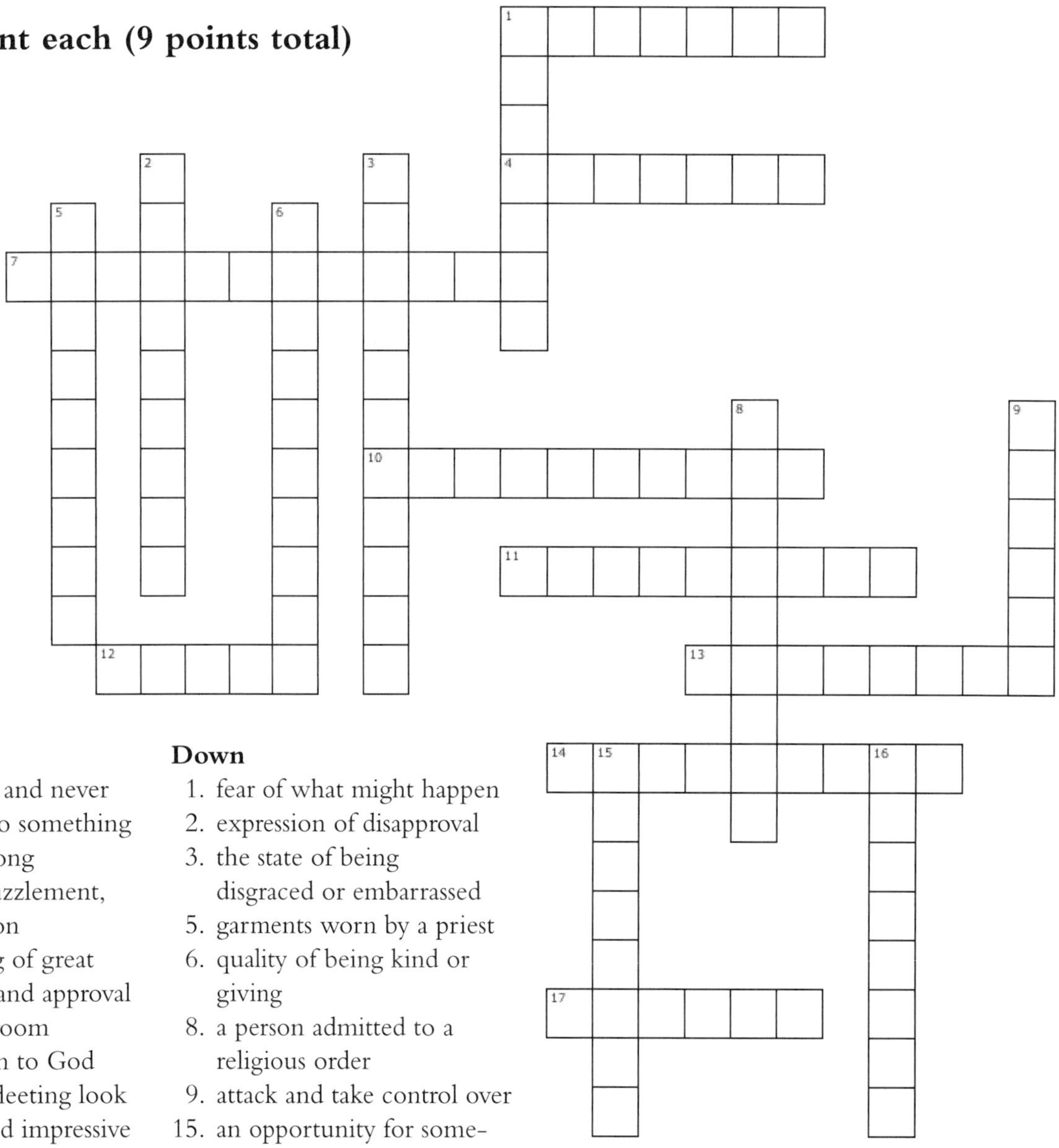

Across

1. to leave and never return to something
4. very strong
7. great puzzlement, confusion
10. a feeling of great respect and approval
11. dining room
12. devotion to God
13. a brief fleeting look
14. great and impressive beauties
17. a strong feeling of excitement

Down

1. fear of what might happen
2. expression of disapproval
3. the state of being disgraced or embarrassed
5. garments worn by a priest
6. quality of being kind or giving
8. a person admitted to a religious order
9. attack and take control over
15. an opportunity for something to happen
16. a consideration paid for the release of someone or something

Key Terms

Match the correct term to its definition.

2 points each (48 points total)

________ a vigil Mass said on Christmas Eve at midnight
________ the prioress at Carmel when Therese entered
________ an order of nuns (Leonie entered this order)
________ someone who died for his or her faith
________ underground tombs in Rome
________ the priest who watched over the affairs of the Carmel community
________ the sub-prioress and novice mistress at Carmel
________ a priest familiar to the Martin family and confessor of Therese
________ the bishop of the diocese of Bayeux and Lisieux who could grant her permission to become a Carmel at a young age
________ a horrible criminal who lived in France at the time
________ a church in Alençon where Louis Martin visited
________ an old nun with rheumatism who needed assistance
________ a small church in Paris where a novena of Masses had been offered for Therese was she was ill
________ a basilica in Paris
________ site of games and entertainments for pagans of ancient Rome
________ a nickname for the city of Rome
________ the pope who Therese met with on her pilgrimage to Rome
________ the old land of Israel
________ a Catholic devotional book that Therese read and loved
________ Therese's name as a Carmelite
________ the day one takes the habit of Carmel and makes a commitment
________ one's solemn and permanent admission into a religious order
________ a female religious order Therese prayed Leonie would enter
________ a place of temporal punishment for those who are not entirely free of venial faults and must pay for their transgressions before entering heaven

A. Basilica of the Sacred Heart
B. bishop of Bayeux
C. Canon Delatroette
D. catacombs
E. Clothing Day
F. Coliseum
G. Eternal City
H. Father Pichon
I. Holy Land
J. martyr
K. Midnight Mass
L. Mother Mary Gonzaga
M. Mother Mary of Angels
N. Notre Dame
O. Our Lady of Victories
P. Poor Clares
Q. Pope Leo XIII
R. Pranzini
S. Purgatory
T. Religious Profession
U. Sister Saint Peter
V. Sister Therese of the Child Jesus
W. The Imitation of Christ
X. Visitation Order

Multiple Choice

Choose the correct response and circle the answer.

3 points each (30 points total)

1. What happened on January 1st, 1888?
   a. Celine was accepted to Carmel.
   b. Louis Martin became a priest.
   c. Therese was accepted to Carmel.
   d. Pauline left Carmel.

2. What did Celine and Therese do when they visited the Coliseum?
   a. They pretended to sword fight.
   b. They were too afraid to enter.
   c. They prayed to the Blessed Virgin.
   d. They kissed the ground to honor the martyrs.

3. What did Celine say to Therese when they discovered they both wanted to go to Carmel?
   a. Celine said she would wait for their father's death.
   b. Celine insisted on going first.
   c. Celine told Therese to find another convent.
   d. Celine decided not to go.

4. Who delayed Therese making her Religious Profession by eight months?
   a. Mother Mary Gonzaga
   b. Canon Delatroette
   c. the pope
   d. Pauline

5. Therese was to stop working in the refectory and was assigned a new task. What was it?
   a. assistant sacristan
   b. cook
   c. infirmary
   d. prioress

6. What did the pope say when Therese asked if she could enter Carmel at fifteen?
   a. yes
   b. it was up to her father
   c. it was up to the superiors
   d. no

7. Who did Therese spend recreation hours with as a novice?
   a. nuns other than her sisters
   b. Pauline
   c. Marie
   d. Pauline and Marie

8. What other vocation did Therese consider?
   a. marriage
   b. a missionary
   c. run an orphanage
   d. live among the homeless

9. What small miracle did Therese pray for on her Clothing Day?
    a. snow
    b. to see the Blessed Virgin
    c. a shower of roses
    d. a rainbow

10. Who became the new prioress in February, 1893?
    a. Therese
    b. Marie
    c. Pauline
    d. Mother Mary Gozaga

Narration Exercise

The remaining 13 points of the quiz will come from this narration exercise. Answer the question below in 2–3 complete sentences.

Which saints did Therese feel a connection with while visiting the Catacombs?

Key Terms

These are important people, places, and things you should remember from this chapter.

The Little Way the method of giving oneself to God as a child (Therese used and taught this to other sisters)

novice a new member of the convent who was seriously discerning the vocation

The Story of a Soul the autobiography written by Therese

Vocabulary

Read the sentences below, and note the use of the word in **bold**. *Write a definition or synonym for this word by considering its context.*

1. I took **refuge** in prayer.

2. This **abandonment** of oneself as a child into the arms of the heavenly Father seemed rather strange advice to some of the novices.

3. The veil now clouding his mind would be gone forever, and we would be united in unending **bliss**.

4. Would she be able to follow such a **rigorous** Rule?

Comprehension Questions

To better understand this chapter, ask yourself these questions, and write down your answers using complete sentences.

1. What did Therese teach the novices?

....

....

....

2. How did Therese use her experience of climbing stairs as a baby to explain the Little Way?

....

....

....

3. Who visited Therese and her sisters at Carmel? Why was it a difficult visit?

....

....

....

4. Why could Celine not go to Carmel right away?

....

....

....

5. After talking with her sisters, what new task was assigned to Therese?

....

....

....

Key Terms

These are important people, places, and things you should remember from this chapter.

Stations of the Cross a way to pray and meditate by contemplating the fourteen stations of Christ's Passion

Society of White Fathers a Catholic missionary society of priests

Sister Mary of the Eucharist the name Therese's cousin, Marie Guerin, took when she entered Carmel

Vocabulary

Read the sentences below, and note the use of the bold word. Write a definition or synonym for this word by considering its context.

1. For some time I prayed and reflected, and then the **inspiration** came.

2. Because of this, death is something to be dreaded and heaven almost impossible of **attainment**.

3. I saw in these young souls the future **welfare** of our monastery.

4. Over and over again I described the beauty and **simplicity** in one's spiritual life.

Comprehension Questions

To better understand this chapter, ask yourself these questions, and write down your answers using complete sentences.

1. What happened on the Feast of the Most Holy Trinity, June 9, 1895?

2. What happened to Therese when she was making the Stations of the Cross?

3. Who did Pauline ask Therese to write letters of encouragement to? Why was this necessary?

4. Which words did Therese often use when teaching about the Little Way?

5. How did Therese explain that feelings do not matter to a novice who questioned the Little Way?

Activity

The following is an optional activity meant to draw you closer to Our Lord's Passion and Crucifixion.

Therese experienced the penetration of a heavenly flame while making the Stations of the Cross.

Make a visit to your church and pray the Stations of the Cross, or locate a book that has them and recite them reverently in your room.

After doing this, write in the name for each station pictured below. Try to do so without the assistance of any books or notes.

The Stations of the Cross:

1

....

....

2

....

....

3

....

....

4

....

....

5

6

7

8

9

10

11

12

13

14

Key Terms

These are important people, places, and things you should remember from this chapter.

repository a side altar in the church where the consecrated Host is reserved from Holy Thursday until Good Friday

Tuberculosis a very serious disease of the lungs

Doctor de Cornière the doctor who attended to the Sisters of Carmel in cases of illness

Doctor La Néele Jane Guerin's husband who was sent to see Therese

Carmel in Hanoi This is where Therese would be sent on a missionary trip in French Indo-China if she recovered.

Mother Anne of Jesus companion of Saint Teresa of Avila and the first to bring the Carmelite Reform to France

Blessed Theophane Venard a holy priest who had died a martyr's death in China

Vocabulary

Read the sentences below and note the use of the word in **bold**. *Write a definition or synonym for this word by considering its context.*

1. I would be strong enough for the **customary** exercises of Good Friday if I spent the whole night in prayer.

2. I left the chapel without **reluctance** and went to pray in my cell.

3. I followed the Good Friday observances with great zest, but after a few hours real **fatigue** came upon me.

4. I reminded Marie, as I have so often reminded the novices, that **pious** feelings are of little importance.

Comprehension Questions

To better understand this chapter, ask yourself these questions, and write down your answers using complete sentences.

1. What happened to Therese on April 3, 1896?

2. What caused the blood that rose to Therese's lips?

3. Although Therese tried to hide her sickness, who was eventually sent to assist her?

4. What other sister asked Therese for a gift? What did she request?

5. Did Therese suffer any doubts or temptations during her illness?

Activity

The following is an optional activity used to help your comprehension of the text. Answer the questions and locate the answers in the Word Search.

1. the day commemorating the Last Supper
2. the day commemorating Christ's death
3. a very serious disease of the lungs
4. the day we celebrate Christ's resurrection
5. a time of prayer, penance, sacrifice, and good works to prepare for the celebration of Christ's resurrection
6. If Therese was to get better, she would go to the Carmel in ____________, in French Indo-China.
7. Therese dreamt about Mother _________ of Jesus and spoke to her in this dream.
8. Mother Anne of Jesus was a companion of Saint _____________ of Avila.
9. Therese had a ______________ against faith which she prayed for the courage to overcome.
10. Therese said, "Grant me _____________ of heart or body!"
11. At the age of fourteen, Therese kissed the holy grounds of ___________.
12. In November 1896, Therese began a novena to Blessed _____________ Venard.

Using your answers to the questions from the opposite page as your word bank, locate the answers within the Word Search.

I	C	X	C	Y	N	D	F	G	Z	D	L	H	Y	Y
Z	R	J	N	C	B	E	I	D	A	N	W	C	A	S
B	Z	S	Y	O	I	T	G	J	G	H	A	F	D	O
E	C	Y	I	M	A	R	T	Y	R	D	O	M	I	R
T	Y	A	D	S	R	U	H	T	Y	L	O	H	R	Y
M	H	X	V	V	O	E	B	T	N	N	Q	E	F	H
T	E	E	Q	E	M	L	E	B	O	E	P	N	D	A
K	A	N	O	O	V	R	U	I	N	Q	L	N	O	V
C	S	R	R	P	E	Q	T	C	V	J	E	A	O	O
A	T	C	C	S	H	A	N	E	R	X	I	D	G	K
C	E	I	A	N	T	A	O	Z	X	E	H	U	V	S
A	R	L	Q	P	I	O	N	A	H	L	B	X	Z	S
P	R	K	M	U	N	O	W	E	H	P	X	U	L	V
N	T	E	F	X	G	P	P	C	W	S	Z	C	T	P
J	T	L	L	P	R	Y	C	K	F	P	P	A	L	E

Note: *Some words may appear backwards.*

Key Terms

These are important people, places, and things you should remember from this chapter.

infirmary the place to care for those who are ill in the Carmelite monastery

Sister Frances Therese Leonie was now known by this name in the Visitation monastery in Caen.

Vocabulary

Read the sentences below, and note the use of the word in **bold**. *Write a definition or synonym for this word by considering its context.*

1. "Well, this little Sister is very **amiable**, but surely she had done nothing much since coming here."

2. I looked quickly at the Sister who was scrubbing so **vigorously** at my side.

3. "Many were the permissions I wanted to ask, and **pretexts** for yielding to my natural affection suggested themselves by the hundreds."

Comprehension Questions

To better understand this chapter, ask yourself these questions, and write down your answers using complete sentences.

1. What did Therese overhear the kitchen sister speaking of outside her cell?

....

....

....

2. What did Pauline ask Therese to do if she felt strong enough?

....

....

....

3. What did Therese write about from Saint Paul's letter to Corinth?

....

....

....

4. To whom did Therese dedicate parts of her book?

....

....

....

5. How did Therese respond when Marie told her there would be great sorrow in the sisters' hearts when she left for heaven?

....

....

....

Activity

The following is an optional activity meant to draw you closer to Holy Scripture.

Therese memorized a passage of Scripture about charity and love.

Read this passage from I Corinthians 13:1-8 below.

Write about how you can develop the virtue of charity and love in your life.

If I speak in the tongues of men and of angels, but have not love, I am a noisy gong or a clanging cymbal. And if I have prophetic powers, and understand all mysteries and all knowledge, and if I have all faith, so as to remove mountains, but have not love, I am nothing. If I give away all I have, and if I deliver my body to be burned, but have not love, I gain nothing.

Love is patient and kind; love is not jealous or boastful; it is not arrogant or rude. Love does not insist on its own way; it is not irritable or resentful; it does not rejoice at wrong, but rejoices in the right. Love bears all things, believes all things, hopes all things, endures all things.

Love never ends; as for prophecies, they will pass away; as for tongues, they will cease; as for knowledge, it will pass away.

Key Terms

These are important people, places, and things you should remember from this chapter.

Sister Genevieve of the Holy Face the name by which Celine was known

Canticle of Canticles an Old Testament Book also known as Song of Songs or Song of Solomon

Vocabulary

Read the sentences below, and note the use of the word in **bold**. *Write a definition or synonym for this word by considering its context.*

1. "If you do otherwise, or if you delay the publication, the Devil will set many snares for you in order to **hinder** God's good work."

2. I feel **incapable** of earning my livelihood, which is Eternal Life.

3. "Later on, they will **enable** you to give pleasure."

4. I had made myself a **victim** for others; God was accepting my offering in its entirety.

Comprehension Questions

To better understand this chapter, ask yourself these questions, and write down your answers using complete sentences.

1. What did Therese receive on July 30th?

2. What did Therese tell Pauline about publishing *The Story of a Soul*?

3. What definition of holiness did Therese give the novices?

4. What role did Celine play at the end of Therese's life?

5. At one point before her death, Therese's suffering became so intense she felt she could not bear it. What did she ask for?

QUIZ 3

Chapters 11–15

Name______________________ Date ____________________ Score_______

Vocabulary

Complete the crossword puzzle using the definitions and synonyms below as clues. All answers will come from the vocabulary sections covered so far. Look back over these sections if you need assistance completing the puzzle. This should be the only part of the quiz where you can view your notes from previous sections.

1 point each (19 points total)

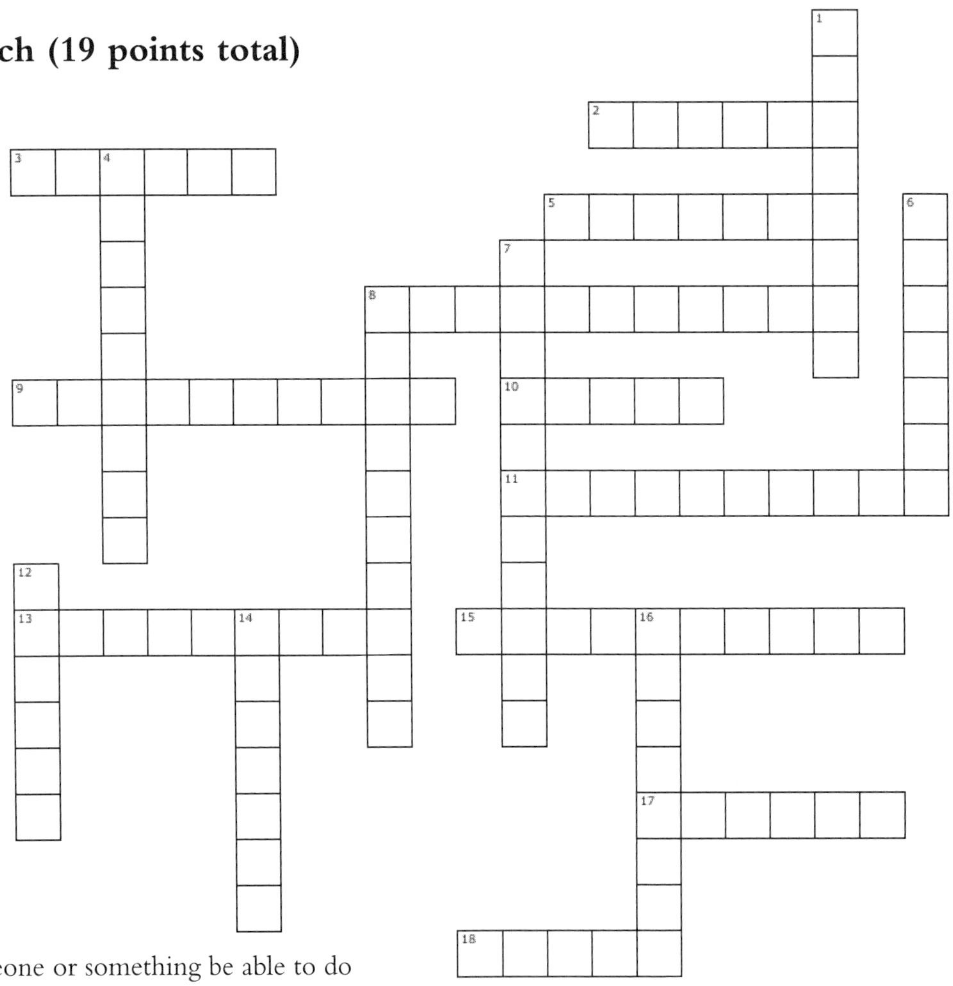

Across

2. to make someone or something be able to do
3. a living being sacrificed to a deity or in the performance of a religious rite
5. weariness from work or exertion
8. self-surrender
9. absence of luxury, plainness
10. devotion to God
11. hesitation
13 not capable
15. done with great force and energy
17. shelter or protection from danger or distress
18. complete happiness

Down

1. excuses
4. usual; habitual
6. well-being
7. a force or influence that inspires someone
8. to reach, obtain
12. to make slow or difficult the progress of
14. friendly and pleasant
16. very strict and demanding

Key Terms

Match the correct term to its definition.

2 points each (34 points total)

________ Therese's method of giving oneself to God as a child

________ a new member of the convent who is seriously discerning the vocation

________ the autobiography Therese wrote

________ a way to pray and meditate on the way of the Cross by contemplating Christ's Passion

________ a Catholic missionary society of priests

________ the name Therese's Cousin, Marie Guerin, took when she entered Carmel

________ a side altar in the church where the consecrated Host is reserved from Holy Thursday until Good Friday

________ a very serious disease of the lungs

________ the doctor who attended the sisters of Carmel in cases of illness

________ Jane Guerin's husband who was sent to treat Therese

________ This is where Therese would be sent on a missionary trip in French Indo-China if she recovered.

________ companion of Saint Teresa of Avila and first to bring the Carmelite Reform to France

________ a holy priest who had died a martyr's death in China

________ the place to care for those who were ill in the Carmelite monastery

________ Leonie was now known by this name in the Visitation monastery in Caen

________ Celine's religious name

________ an Old Testament Book also known as Song of Songs or Song of Solomon

A. Blessed Theophane Venard
B. Canticle of Canticles
C. Carmel in Hanoi
D. Doctor de Cornière
E. Doctor La Néele
F. infirmary
G. Mother Anne of Jesus
H. novice
I. Sister Frances Therese
J. Sister Genevieve of the Holy Face
K. Sister Mary of the Eucharist
L. repository
M. Society of White Fathers
N. The Little Way
O. The Stations of the Cross
P. The Story of a Soul
Q. Tuberculosis

QUIZ 3

Chapters 11–15

Multiple Choice

Choose the correct response and circle the answer.

3 points each (30 points total)

1. Why did the infirmarian sprinkle Holy Water around Therese's bed?
   a. to fight the Devil
   b. to cure Therese
   c. to summon the Blessed Virgin
   d. to cool Therese

2. From which illness did Therese suffer that eventually led to her death?
   a. measles
   b. tuberculosis
   c. influenza
   d. bronchitis

3. What great virtue did Therese write about in her book just before her death?
   a. hope
   b. faith
   c. prudence
   d. charity

4. When Pauline was prioress, what special task did she request from Therese?
   a. to write down the story of her life
   b. to take art lessons
   c. to go on a missionary trip
   d. to fast daily

5. What did Therese experience while making the Stations of the Cross?
   a. the stigmata
   b. a vision of Christ
   c. a penetration of a heavenly flame
   d. a vision of Saint Teresa of Avila

6. What job did Celine have at Carmel at the end of Therese's life?
   a. prioress
   b. assistant sacristan
   c. assistant infirmarian
   d. missionary

7. What did Therese tell Marie would happen after she had died?
   a. it would snow
   b. there would be a shower of roses
   c. there would be a shower of lilies
   d. there would be a choir of angels

8. Who did Therese dream about and talk with to learn about her time left on earth?
   a. Mother Anne of Jesus
   b. her mother
   c. Christ
   d. Saint Paul

9. Leonie was the only sister who was not at Carmel. What was her vocation?
   a. marriage
   b. a missionary
   c. single life
   d. joined the Visitation order

10. Who did Therese first write letters of encouragement to?
   a. cousin Jane
   b. Celine
   c. a seminarian missionary
   d. a Carmel novice

Narration Exercise

The remaining 17 points of the quiz will come from this narration exercise. Answer the question below in 2–3 complete sentences.

How did Therese choose a title for her autobiography?

Essay

To be written after completion of the novel and all quizzes. Graded at parent's discretion.

Explain why St. Therese became a saint, and what virtues she displayed throughout the course of her life. In what ways can you emulate her in your everyday life so that you too can practice these virtues?

Glossary

Act of Consecration the solemn dedication Therese made to give herself and all her actions and deeds to the Blessed Virgin

Alençon the city in France where the Martin family lived

Aunt Celine married to Isidore; aunt to the Martin girls

Basilica of the Sacred Heart a Basilica in Paris

Benedictine convent the place where Therese went to study just before the age of nine.

Bishop of Bayeux the bishop of the diocese of Bayeux and Lisieux who could grant her permission to become a Carmelite at a young age

Blessed Theophane Venard a holy priest who had died a martyr's death in China

Bluebeard a make-believe person whom frightened Therese

Canon Delatroette the priest who watched over the affairs of the Carmel community

Canticle of Canticles an Old Testament Book also known as Song of Songs or Song of Solomon

Carmel in Hanoi This is where Therese would be sent on a missionary trip in French Indo-China if she recovered.

Carmelite nun a cloistered nun who lives with her community inside walls apart from the rest of the world

Catacombs underground tombs in Rome

Clothing Day the day one takes the habit of Carmel and makes a commitment

Coliseum site of games and entertainments for the pagans of ancient Rome

Doctor de Cornière the doctor who attended the sisters of Carmel in cases of illness

Doctor La Néele Jane Guerin's husband who was sent to see Therese

Eternal City a nickname for the city of Rome

Father Domin the Benedictine convent chaplain

Father Pichon a priest familiar to the Martin Family and confessor of Therese

first Holy Communion the sacrament of receiving Jesus in the Eucharist for the first time

hermit a person who lives in seclusion from the rest of the world

Holy Land the old land of Israel

infirmary the place to care for those who were ill in the Carmelite monastery

Isidore Guerin Zelie's brother; a chemist; the Martin girls' uncle

Last Sacraments final sacraments received by a Catholic before dying including Confession, receiving the Eucharist, and Extreme Unction

Les Buissonnets new home to the Martin family meaning "a wooded estate," also referred to as The Elms

Les Mans the city where the boarding school the Martin girls went to was located

Lisieux the city where Zelie's brother lived

Lisieux the place the Martin family moved after the death of their mother

Louis Joseph Aloysius Stanislaus Martin Therese's father

Lourdes the place Therese's mother and sisters made a pilgrimage to asking Mary to intercede for their mother's health

martyr someone who died for his or her faith

Memorare a prayer to the Blessed Virgin Mary

Midnight Mass a vigil mass said on Christmas Eve at midnight

Mother Anne of Jesus companion of Saint Teresa of Avila and first to bring the Carmelite Reform to France

Mother Mary Gonzaga the prioress at Carmel

Mother Mary of Angels the sub-prioress and novice mistress at Carmel

Notre Dame a church in Alençon where Louis Martin visited

novice a new member of the convent who was seriously discerning the vocation

Our Lady of Victories a small church in Paris where a novena of Masses had been offered for Therese while she was ill

Poor Clares an order of nuns. Leonie entered this order.

Pope Leo XIII the pope whom Therese met with on her pilgrimage to Rome

Pranzini a horrible criminal who lived in France at the time

purgatory a place of temporal punishment for those who are not entirely free of venial sins and must pay for their transgressions before entering heaven

Religious Profession one's solemn and permanent admission into a religious order.

repository a side altar in the Church where the consecrated Host is reserved from Holy Thursday until Good Friday

Rose Taillé the woman who took care of baby Therese and who the baby mistook for her mother

Sacrament of Confirmation the sacrament of renewing one's baptismal promises and having the Holy Spirit leading a firm profession of faith

Sister Agnes of Jesus the name Pauline took when she became a Carmelite nun

Sister Frances Therese Leonie was now known by this name in the Visitation monastery in Caen

Sister Genevieve of the Holy Face the name Celine was now known as

Sister Mary Dosithée Zelie's sister who was at the Visitation convent and passed away before Zelie became sick

Sister Mary of the Eucharist the name Therese's Cousin, Marie Guerin, took when she entered Carmel

Sister Saint Peter an old nun with rheumatism who needed assistance

Sister Therese of the Child Jesus Therese's name as a Carmelite

Society of White Fathers a catholic missionary society of priests

Stations of the Cross a way to pray and meditate on the way of the cross by contemplating on fourteen different stations from the time Christ was condemned to His burial

The Imitation of Christ a catholic devotional book Therese read and loved

The Little Way the method of giving oneself to God as a child Therese used and taught to other sisters

The Story of a Soul the autobiography Therese wrote

Tuberculosis a very serious disease of the lungs

Victoria a maid of the Martin family

Visitation convent the boarding school Marie and Pauline attended

Visitation Order a female religious order Therese prayed Leonie would enter

watchmaker the profession of Therese's father

Zelie Marie Guerin Therese's mother

Notes

Notes

More Great Titles From Neumann Press

The Catechism comes to life with these timeless stories!

Father Gerald T. Brennan

This collection of Fr. Brennan's short sermons and engaging stories will entertain young readers and impart delightful lessons of truth. Each volume includes a topical section at the end relating main subjects of the stories to chapters in the Baltimore Catechism. Volume 1 includes: *The Devil at the Door*, *Marty's First Mass*, *The Girl in the Shabby Dress*, and *The Boy Who Made God Smile.*

978-0-91184-566-2 • Hardcover

Angel Food for Boys & Girls Volume II

Includes: *The Orphan's Plea*, *A Surprise for a King*, *Half Past Three*, and more.

978-0-91184-567-9

Hardcover

Angel Food for Boys & Girls Volume III

Includes: *Is God Very Big?*, *Jesus! Are You There?*, *A Mother's Note*, and more.

978-0-91184-594-5

Hardcover

Angel Food for Boys & Girls Volume IV

Includes: *St. Peter Goes Shopping*, *The Priest of Times Square*, *Jesus' Workshop.*

978-0-91184-595-2

Hardcover

NeumannPress.com • (800) 437-5876

TAN · BOOKS

TAN Books was founded in 1967 to preserve the spiritual, intellectual and liturgical traditions of the Catholic Church. At a critical moment in history TAN kept alive the great classics of the Faith and drew many to the Church. In 2008 TAN was acquired by Saint Benedict Press. Today TAN continues its mission to a new generation of readers.

From its earliest days TAN has published a range of booklets that teach and defend the Faith. Through partnerships with organizations, apostolates, and mission-minded individuals, well over 10 million TAN booklets have been distributed.

More recently, TAN has expanded its publishing with the launch of Catholic calendars and daily planners—as well as Bibles, fiction, and multimedia products through its sister imprints Catholic Courses (CatholicCourses.com) and Saint Benedict Press (SaintBenedictPress.com). In 2015, TAN Homeschool became the latest addition to the TAN family, preserving the Faith for the next generation of Catholics (www.TANHomeschool.com).

Today TAN publishes over 500 titles in the areas of theology, prayer, devotions, doctrine, Church history, and the lives of the saints. TAN books are published in multiple languages and found throughout the world in schools, parishes, bookstores and homes.